In Times Long

Sing to the tune of "The Wheels on the Bus"

The children long ago worked on chores,
Worked on chores, worked on chores.

The children long ago worked on chores,
In times long ago.

They fed the hens and gathered eggs,
Gathered eggs, gathered eggs.

They fed the hens and gathered eggs,
In times long ago.

They worked in the garden to grow their food,
6 Grow their food, grow their food.

They worked in the garden to grow their food,
In times long ago.

They gathered wood to build a fire,
Build a fire, build a fire.

They gathered wood to build a fire,
In times long ago.

They milked the cow for milk to drink,
Milk to drink, milk to drink.

They milked the cow for milk to drink,
In times long ago.

They churned the butter for the bread,
For the bread, for the bread.

They churned the butter for the bread,
In times long ago.

The children long ago worked on chores,
Worked on chores, worked on chores.

14

The children long ago worked on chores,
In times long ago.

The children of today do chores, too.
Do chores, too, do chores, too.
The children of today do chores, too.
Just like long ago!